Write It Right

Writing a Memoir

By Cecilia Minden

Published in the United States of America by
CHERRY LAKE PRESS
Ann Arbor, Michigan, 2395 South Huron Parkway, Suite 200
www.cherrylakepublishing.com

Reading Adviser: Marla Conn, MS, Ed., Literacy specialist, Read-Ability, Inc.
Book Designer: Felicia Macheske
Character Illustrator: Carol Herring

Photo Credits: © Erickson Stock/Shutterstock.com, 5; © JGA/Shutterstock.com, 11; © KK Tan/Shutterstock.com, 13;
© Monkey Business Images/Shutterstock.com, 15; © Rawpixel.com/Shutterstock.com, 19

Graphics Throughout: © simple surface/Shutterstock.com; © Mix3r/Shutterstock.com; © Artefficient/Shutterstock.com; © lemony/
Shutterstock.com; © Svetolk/Shutterstock.com; © EV-DA/Shutterstock.com; © briddy/Shutterstock.com; © IreneArt/Shutterstock.com

Library of Congress Cataloging-in-Publication Data

Names: Minden, Cecilia, author. | Herring, Carol, illustrator.
Title: Writing a memoir / by Cecilia Minden ; illustrated by Carol Herring.

Description: Ann Arbor, Michigan : Cherry Lake Publishing, [2020] |
 Series: Write it right | Includes bibliographical references and index. |
 Audience: Grades: 2-3
Identifiers: LCCN 2019033387 (print) | LCCN 2019033388 (ebook)
 | ISBN 9781534159044 (hardcover) | ISBN 9781534161344 (paperback)
 | ISBN 9781534160194 (pdf) | ISBN 9781534162495 (ebook)
Subjects: LCSH: Autobiography—Authorship—Juvenile literature.
Classification: LCC CT25 .M494 2020 (print) | LCC CT25 (ebook) | DDC
 808.06/692—dc23
LC record available at https://lccn.loc.gov/2019033387
LC ebook record available at https://lccn.loc.gov/2019033388

Cherry Lake Publishing would like to acknowledge the work of the Partnership for 21st Century Learning, a Network of Battelle
for Kids. Please visit www.battelleforkids.org/networks/p21 for more information.

Printed in the United States of America
Corporate Graphics

CHERRY LAKE PRESS

Table of
CONTENTS

CHAPTER ONE

Let's Talk About You!

Do you like to listen to your family tell stories? It is fun to know about their experiences. A good way to remember your own experiences is to write a **memoir**.

A memoir is an **account** of your personal experiences. You can write a memoir about your entire life. You could also just write about certain parts of it. You don't have to be famous or old to write a memoir. Everyone has stories to tell about their lives.

Writing your memoir can be a lot of fun. Think about some of your most fun memories. Think about picnics at a park or playing games with friends in your backyard.

Check your family photo albums for inspiration.

CHAPTER TWO

Stories of Your Life

A memoir is like any good story. It needs three basic parts. These parts are characters, settings, and an interesting **plot**. You should also mix in some **conflict**. Maybe you got lost on a field trip or didn't have enough money to buy your lunch. A little humor and even some sadness will make your stories more interesting.

The plot of your memoir is the action and the events that make up your life. You might write about moving to a new town. You could describe what it is like to change schools and make new friends.

An example of a favorite memory would be getting a new pet.

Who will be the main character in your memoir? You! You have years of memories. You know what makes you happy and sad and what you wish for the future. Other characters in your memoir can include your family and friends. You could even write about your pets!

Settings are the locations of your story. They could include your home, school, or favorite restaurant. They could also include places you've visited, like a big city or the beach.

Here's what you'll need to complete the activities in this book:

- Pencil
- Ruler
- Notebook paper

ACTIVITY

Reviewing a Story

It is often helpful to think back on stories other people have told you. In this activity, you will describe what it was like to listen to someone else tell a story about his or her life. The story can come from anyone, including a relative or a friend.

INSTRUCTIONS:

1. Write the name of the storyteller and the subject of the story at the top of a sheet of paper.

2. Use a ruler to help you make three boxes.

3. Label one box "What Made the Story Memorable?" Label the second box "Were They a Good Storyteller?" Label the last box "Which of Their Storytelling Skills Do I Have?"

4. Fill in the boxes of your chart with your thoughts about the experience you had with your storyteller.

Storyteller's Name: Charley, my older cousin
Subject of Story: Teaching in a one-room school

What Made the Story Memorable?

- Interesting characters, such as Charley's friend Marco.
- The setting, a one-room school in the hills of New Mexico. It was winter and really cold.
- The way Charley told the story. He described the setting in detail.

Were They a Good Storyteller?

- Charley is a good storyteller because he is funny and remembers lots of details to make the story interesting.
- He got me involved in his story. He made me feel almost like I was with him in the one-room school with a wood stove to keep us warm.
- When he told me sad parts of his story, he showed he cared about the other characters.

Which of Their Storytelling Skills Do I Have?

- I give lots of details about people and places when I tell a story.
- I can tell a story with lots of emotion to make it interesting.
- I like sharing parts of my life with others.

CHAPTER THREE

So Many Memories

Where do you get the material that you'll need to tell your life story? You simply begin by jogging your memory. Do some creative **brainstorming**!

Think about people you've met and places you've visited. Recall events you have attended. Think about the important people or situations that have shaped your life. Your life would be very different without these people or events.

Try looking through family photo albums and pictures saved on your family computer. Who are the people in the photos? Do you know them? How? Are you in any of the photos? Where were the photos taken? What were you doing there? Ask other relatives to help you remember the faces.

Your first time riding a bike would be
an important memory to include!

Make Lists

You will make two memory lists in this activity. One will be a list of people, places, events, thoughts, or feelings. The second list will be major events in your life that shaped who you are.

INSTRUCTIONS:

1. Use a ruler to help you make two columns.

2. Write "Memory Lists" at the top of the page.

3. Write "My Memories" at the top of the left-hand column. Write "My Major Events" at the top of the right-hand column.

4. Fill in the chart with your personal memories.

MY MEMORIES

- My first day of school
- Family dinners at our favorite restaurant
- Playing soccer
- Learning to ride a bike
- Making pizza with my sister ✔
- Sleigh ride on Christmas Eve
- Summers at the beach
- Storytime at the library

MY MAJOR EVENTS

- When Grandpa came to live with us
- When my big sister went away to college
- When we adopted our dog

CHAPTER FOUR

Make It Real for Others

Now you have all you need to write an interesting memoir. You could begin your memoir by describing the very beginning of your life. You could also start with a joke or even a shocking fact about your life.

Start each new memory on a separate sheet of notebook paper. You can also type your memories on a computer. It is easier to write many short stories instead of one long story. You can rearrange the stories when you do the final edit of your memoir.

Begin with memories that will catch your reader's attention.

Using a computer will make it easier to rearrange
memories into a different order or to add new details.

Take time to describe the characters and settings of each memory. How did something taste and look? How did it sound and feel? How did someone speak? What unusual habits do your characters have? Add details to help your stories mean as much to your readers as they do to you.

A story about learning to bowl might describe the bowling alley and the person helping you.

Practice Writing

This activity will help you practice writing a chapter in your memoir. You can go back later to add in more details.

INSTRUCTIONS:

1. Choose a memory.
2. Write the events of that memory in the order they occurred.
3. Add details. Think about colors, sounds, and smells.
4. You can go back later and add more details as you remember them.

Sample Memoir Story

My big sister and I love making homemade pizzas for dinner. This time, however, the dough was too thin to spread across the whole pan. Then my sister had an idea. She said we could make individual pizzas instead. The dough was just enough to make four personal pizzas. This way was a lot better because we could use any toppings we wanted! I put lots of pepperoni slices on mine. My sister put olives on her pizza—yuck!

CHAPTER FIVE

Final Polish

Now it's time to organize your stories. Here are a few different ways to do this:

Organize by time. You could put your earliest childhood memory first. Then you would place memories by your age. Organizing your stories by time is an easy way for people to follow your memoir.

Organize by subject. If you organize your memoir by subject, you might put everything about school in one chapter. Stories about holidays could go in a separate chapter. You could even divide them by seasons: fall, winter, spring, and summer.

Organize by theme. A theme is the main idea of a piece of writing. You could organize your memoir by stories about friendship, overcoming fears, or learning how to do new things.

Ask a friend or teacher to read your
memoir and give you feedback.

After you are finished writing, take time to read through your memoir. Are your characters, settings, and actions described in detail? Do the connections between the stories make sense? Are your stories interesting to other people? It may be necessary to rewrite parts of your memoir to make it the best it can be.

By writing your memoir, you've explored your life and the lives of people who you care most about. You've taken an exciting step toward discovering yourself!

Edit Your Memoir

Ask yourself these questions as you reread your memoir:

- Are the names of people and their relationships to me clear?
- Is it clear where and when the memories took place?
- Have I described characters, settings, and actions with enough detail?
- Are all the words in my memoir spelled correctly?
- Have I used correct punctuation throughout my memoir?
- Have I grouped similar memories together into longer sections?
- Do the connections between the individual stories make sense?
- Have I used dialogue throughout my memoir?

GLOSSARY

account (uh-KOUNT) a description of something that has happened

brainstorming (BRAYN-storm-ing) thinking hard to try to come up with ideas or solutions

conflict (KAHN-flikt) a struggle or disagreement

memoir (MEM-wahr) an account of an author's personal experiences

plot (PLAHT) the main story of a memoir or a work of fiction

BOOKS

Kalman, Bobbie. *I Can Write a Book about My Life*. New York, NY: Crabtree Publishing, 2012.

Kamberg, Mary-Lane. *The I Love to Write Book: Ideas & Tips for Young Writers*. Milwaukee, WI: Crickhollow Books, 2008.

WEBSITES

Creative Writing Now—How to Write a Memoir
www.creative-writing-now.com/how-to-write-a-memoir.html
Find advice on how to write a memoir, as well as interviews and ideas to inspire your memoir writing.

Scholastic—Brainstorm: Memoirs from Life
http://teacher.scholastic.com/writeit/memoir/brainstorm/fromlife.htm
Use these prompts to help you think of where to start on your memoir. Check out some useful tips that will help you complete any writing project.

INDEX

About the AUTHOR

Cecilia Minden is the former director of the Language and Literacy Program at Harvard Graduate School of Education. She earned her doctorate from the University of Virginia. While at Harvard, Dr. Minden also taught several writing courses. Her research focused on early literacy skills and developing phonics curriculums. She is now a literacy consultant and the author of over 200 books for children. Dr. Minden lives with her family in McKinney, Texas. She enjoys helping students become interested in reading and writing.